LOOK AT
FEET

First published in the USA by

Franklin Watts Inc
387 Park Avenue South
New York 10016

ISBN: 0−531−10615−2
Library of Congress
Catalog Card No: 88−50573

Design: David Bennett
Illustrations: Julia Osorno
Editor: Ruth Thomson

Printed in Italy
by G. Canale & C. S.p.A. Turin

The author and publisher would
like to thank the following people
for allowing their feet to be bared
for photography: Su Walton, Peter
Millard, Melissa Case, Sarah Knight,
Leo Thomson, Tyrone Watkins, Nicola
Hickmann-Robertson, Chloe Thomson.
James Green, Ursula Hageli, Rosa Curling.

Shoes and boots courtesy of Clarks,
sports equipment kindly loaned by
Lillywhites, tap shoes loaned by
Anello and Davide, pedal and footpump
courtesy of Angel Motors

Additional photographs:
Colorsport: pages 22, 23;
Science Photo Library: page 13;
John Watney: page 28

LOOK AT
FEET

Henry Pluckrose
Photography by Mike Galletly

FRANKLIN WATTS
London · New York · Sydney · Toronto

Have you ever looked closely at feet? Feet on which we stand…

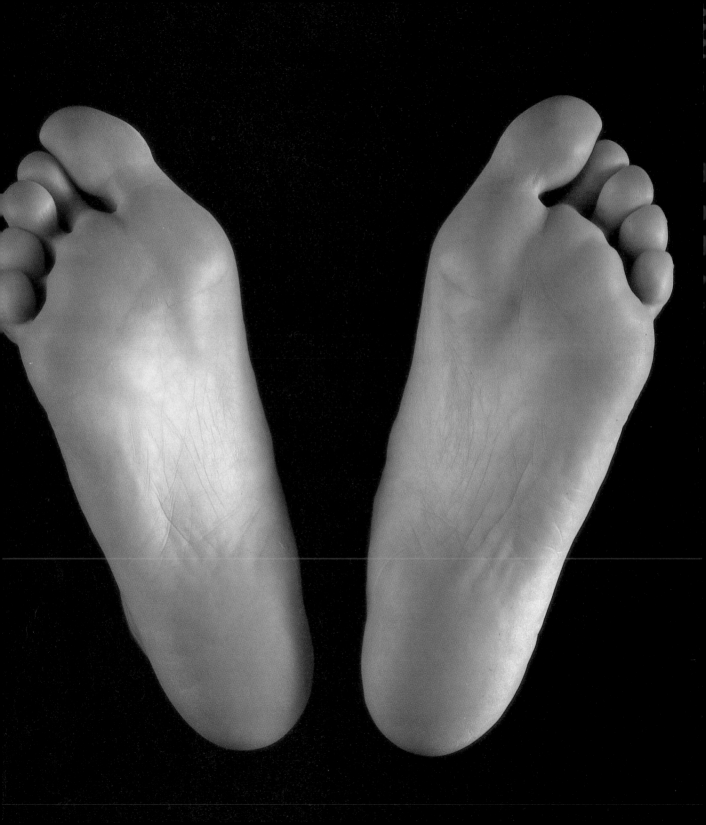

with which we walk...

run…

and climb.
We could hardly manage
without them.

When we move,
we use our toes
as well as our heels.

Look at your toes.
Can you move them
in as many ways as
your fingers and thumbs?

Choose some objects like these.
How many can you pick up
with your toes?
Which shapes and textures
are easiest to grasp?

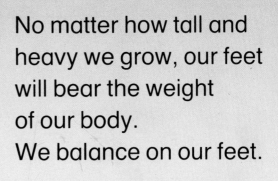

No matter how tall and heavy we grow, our feet will bear the weight of our body.
We balance on our feet.

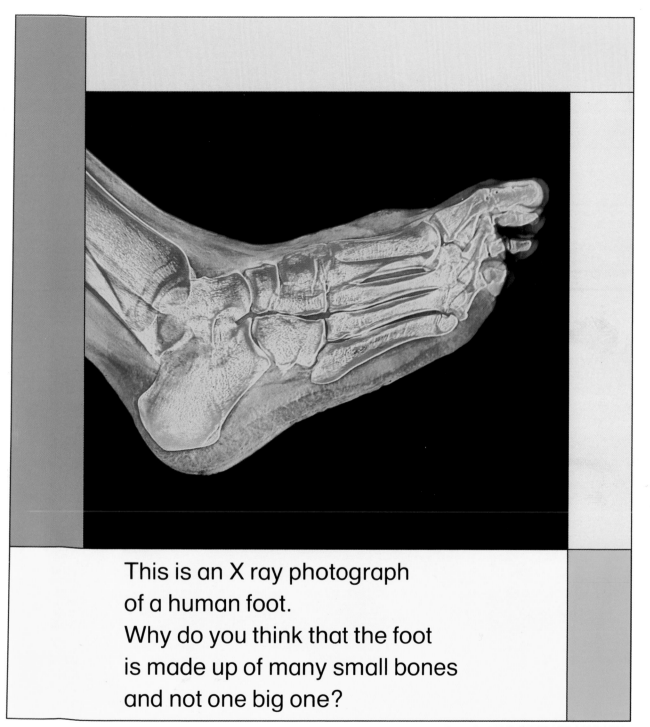

This is an X ray photograph
of a human foot.
Why do you think that the foot
is made up of many small bones
and not one big one?

People use their feet to do many different things –

to pump up a tire . . .

or to slow down a car,

to pedal the wheels
of a bicycle . . .

or to play a piano!

We use our feet for dancing.
This ballet dancer moves
gracefully on point –
the very tips of her toes.

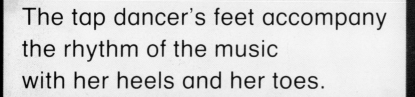

The tap dancer's feet accompany
the rhythm of the music
with her heels and her toes.

We use our feet to take part in all sorts of sports.
Do you know for which sports these things are used?

How else can we use
our feet? Where might
you see people…

kicking a ball?

hanging from
their insteps?

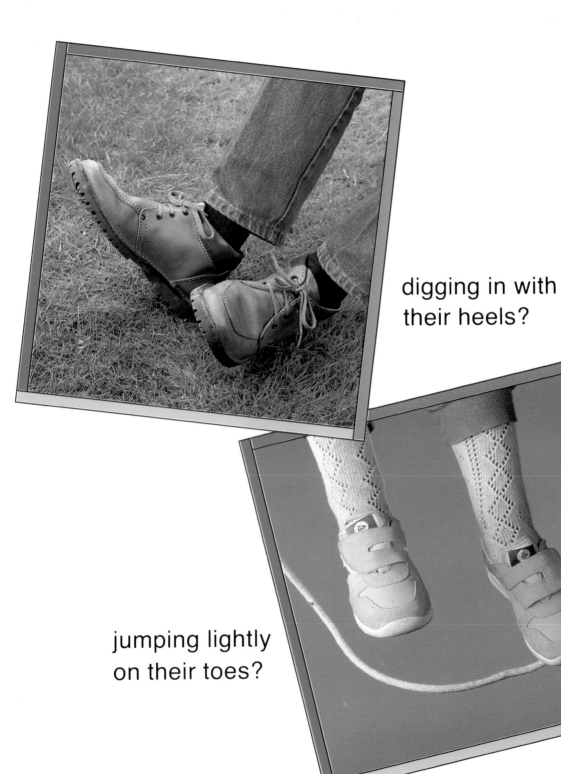

digging in with
their heels?

jumping lightly
on their toes?

A runner's feet
touch the ground
at least 50,000 times
in a marathon race.

For some people
this can be too many!

Touch the sole of your foot. The skin is soft and tender. It is difficult to run across a stony beach in bare feet.

Put on a blindfold and
see how well you can identify
different textures with your feet.

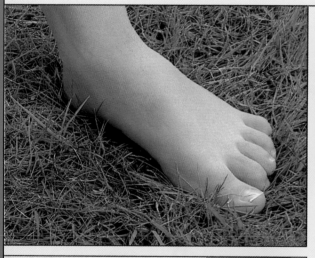

We protect our feet by wearing shoes and sandals.

We keep them warm by wearing slippers and boots.

Some people cannot use
their legs and feet.
How do they manage to move about?

Do you know?

● You have 26 bones in each of your feet. Fourteen of them are in your toes. The largest bone is the one in the heel. The bones move so that you can walk on uneven surfaces. The bones are held together with strong bands of tissue, called ligaments.

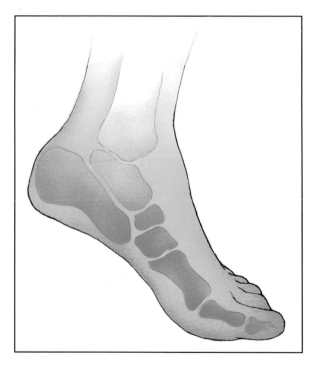

● The sole of your foot has the thickest skin of your body. It also has more sweat glands than any other part of your body, apart from the palms of your hands.

● The bones in your feet continue to grow until you reach the age of 18. They grow particularly quickly when you are a baby and during adolescence. This is why it is important to wear shoes that fit properly.

   If you wear shoes that are too tight or ones that are too big, so that your toes curl under to grip, your feet can become distorted.

● In early times, parts of the body were used as units of length. The *foot* was the length of the tip of the big toe to the back of the heel. Three foot lengths (heel to toe, heel to toe, heel to toe) were the same as one *yard*.

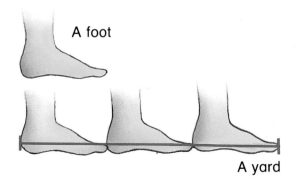

A foot

A yard

Things to do

● Measure your classroom or bedroom in foot lengths. Compare your measurements with those of your friends. Are they the same?

Why do you think that "one foot length" has been replaced by standardized measures (like those found on meter rulers)?

● Using two thin strips of cardboard or paper, measure both feet. Mark one strip "right foot" and the other "left foot." Which foot is the longer? Measure the feet of your friends in a similar way and make a chart of your findings. Do most people have a longer right or left foot?

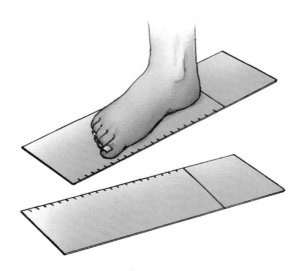

● What is the area of the sole of your foot? Take off a shoe and sock. Put your bare foot on a sheet of graph paper. Carefully draw around it on the paper with a pencil.

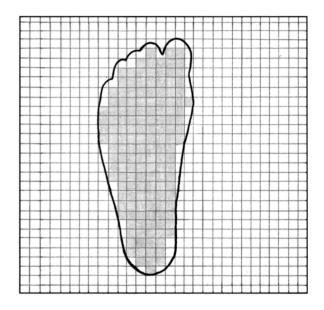

Color and number all the whole squares (1, 2, 3, 4 etc.). Now estimate how many more whole squares you could make from the part squares that remain. Add this number to your whole square total.

This will give you a reasonably accurate figure, squared, of the area of your foot.

● Find some fine sand and put it in a tray or a shallow cardboard box. Dampen the surface so that it is smooth. Gently press your foot into the sand to leave a deep impression.

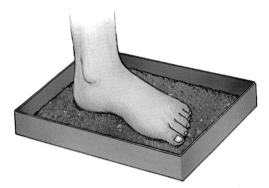

Mix some dental or superfine builder's plaster with water. Pour this into the footprint, lightly tapping the sides of the tray to spread the plaster. Let it harden.

When it is dry, remove the plaster cast of your foot, brushing off any excess sand. The sand can be used again to make any number of casts.

Words about feet

Have you ever thought how often the word *foot* occurs in the English language? Can you add to this list?

football
footbridge
footfall
foothill
foothold
footman
footnote
footpath
footprint
footrest

foot soldier
footsore
footstool
footwear
footwork

Sayings about feet

There are lots of sayings about feet. Can you find out what these ones mean?

To set someone on his feet
To fall on one's feet
To put one's foot in it
To hot foot it
To have one foot in the grave
To be footloose
To throw oneself at a person's feet
To come on foot
To be beneath one's feet

Index

DATE DUE

FF 21 '92			
MR 17 '92			
JE 19 '92			
MAR 21 '94			
JI 14 98			